WHAT'S SO SCARY ABOUT
SHARKS

Joanne Mattern

RED
CHAIR
· PRESS ·

What's So Scary is produced and published by Red Chair Press:

Red Chair Press LLC   PO Box 333   South Egremont, MA 01258-0333
www.redchairpress.com

FREE Educator Guides at www.redchairpress.com/free-resources

Publisher's Cataloging-In-Publication Data

Names: Mattern, Joanne, 1963- author. | Mattern, Joanne, 1963- Earth's
    amazing animals.
Title: What's so scary about sharks? / Joanne Mattern.

Description: South Egremont, MA : Red Chair Press, [2022] | Series: Core
    content science : Earth's amazing animals | Interest age level:
    008-010. | Includes index and suggested resources for further reading.
    | Summary: "Although some sharks are very scary and dangerous, most
    species are quiet creatures who pose no threat to humans at all.
    Readers will learn all about the many kinds of sharks, what they eat,
    where they live, and their importance to the ocean ecosystem in this
    fact-and-photo-packed look at one of nature's top predators"--Provided
    by publisher.

Identifiers: ISBN 9781643711652 (hardcover) | ISBN 9781643711690
    (softcover) | ISBN 9781643711737 (ePDF) | ISBN 9781643711775 (ePub 3
    S&L) | ISBN 9781643711812 (ePub 3 TR) | ISBN 9781643711850 (Kindle)

Subjects: LCSH: Sharks--Juvenile literature. | CYAC: Sharks.

Classification: LCC QL638.9 .M38 2022 (print) | LCC QL638.9 (ebook) | DDC
    597.3--dc23

Library of Congress Control Number: 2021945361

Photo credits: Cover, p. 1, 3, 5, 6, 7, 15, 18, 19, 21, 22, 25, 26, 28: iStock; p. 4, 8–14,
16, 17, 20, 23, 24, 30, back cover: Shutterstock

Printed in United States of America
0422 1P CGF22

Table of Contents

Scary Sharks!

A shadow glides quickly through the water. A sharp fin pokes up from the waves. Huge jaws filled with sharp teeth come closer and closer. You scream and run out of the water. It's a shark attack!

Many people are scared of sharks. Are sharks scary? Yes. These animals are big **predators**. Sometimes they attack people. But sharks are also very important to life on Earth. And most sharks are completely harmless to people. Let's learn about these kings of the sea and why many sharks are not so scary.

A Great white shark like this
one was the type featured
in the 1975 movie "*Jaws*".

Gills

Shark Basics

Sharks are fish. Like all fish, sharks live in water. They do not breathe air like land animals do. Instead, sharks get oxygen from water that passes over their **gills**.

Sharks have eight senses. They have the senses of sight, hearing, touch, smell, and taste; the same five senses humans have. They also have three special senses that help them feel motion in the water. One sense helps them pick up electrical signals from other fish.

Now You Know!

There are more than 500 species of shark. The largest is the whale shark. This shark can be up to 39 feet (12 meters) long. One of the smallest is the dwarf lantern shark. It is just eight inches (20 cm) long.

Sharks live in oceans all over the world. Some live in the warm waters of the Pacific and Indian Oceans. Others live in the colder Atlantic Ocean. Some sharks even live in the icy Arctic Ocean.

Shark Bodies

Most fish bodies are made of bones. Not sharks! Their bodies are made of a tough material called **cartilage**. You have cartilage too. It's found in your nose and ears.

A shark's skin feels very rough. Shark skin is made of tiny scales. These scales have spikes that point backward toward the shark's tail. Water flows smoothly around the spikes. This helps the shark swim quickly and quietly.

Most shark bodies are perfectly shaped for swimming. Their bodies are narrow at the head and tail. They are thicker in the middle. This shape helps them swim fast.

Most sharks are cold-blooded. But a few, like the great white, can keep some parts of their bodies warm. This helps them move fast.

Sharks have great eyesight. They also have a very strong sense of smell and can sense even a tiny amount of blood in the water.

Sharks have lots of teeth. They use them to rip chunks of flesh from their **prey**. A shark's teeth fall out all the time, but not to worry! A shark has many rows of teeth in its mouth. When one tooth falls out, another moves up to take its place.

A shark's mouth is made for catching prey. Some shark teeth point backward. That helps the shark get a good grip on its dinner. A shark can also unhinge its jaws. That lets it open its mouth extra-wide!

What's For Dinner?

Sharks are apex predators. That means they are at the top of the food chain. Sharks eat many different things, but most animals don't prey on sharks.

Great white sharks eat large fish, stingrays, seals, dolphins, and other big animals. Other sharks, like the tiger shark or bull shark, eat sea turtles or birds.

Not all sharks eat big prey. Horn sharks crush lobsters and crabs with their flat, strong teeth. The megamouth shark **filters** tiny sea creatures out of the water with its big mouth.

An orca, or killer whale, is probably the only animal, besides humans, that can kill a big shark.

Shark Friends

You might think fish are scared of sharks. After all, they could be the shark's next meal! But some fish choose to swim near sharks. Small pilot fish swim with sharks to stay safe. They know that most big fish will stay far away from the shark. That keeps the pilot fish safe too.

Remora fish use a sucker to attach themselves to a shark. These fish actually help the shark. They eat **parasites** off the shark's skin and in its mouth. They also eat bits of food that the shark drops.

Pilot fish stay with a shark for protection.

Baby Sharks

Most sharks give birth to live young. Baby sharks are called pups. A great white shark has one or two pups at a time. Other sharks can have more than 20 pups at one time.

When a baby shark is born, it is still attached to its mother by a long cord. That cord soon breaks. Then the pup swims off. It can take care of itself right away.

Some sharks lay lots of leathery eggs. They hide the eggs in a safe place. A few months later, the baby sharks hatch and swim away.

Now You Know!

Sometimes people find the cases that held shark eggs. These cases are called mermaid's purses.

Meet the Sharks

Here are a few of the many **species** of sharks on Planet Earth:

Great White Shark

The great white is a large and dangerous shark. It lives in cool waters off the coast. Great whites can swim up to 37 miles (60 km) per hour. They feed on large animals, like seals.

Great white shark

Hammerhead shark

Hammerhead Shark

The hammerhead could win a prize for Weirdest Looking Fish! This shark gets its name from its odd-shaped head. A hammerhead shark's eyes are so far apart, they can see in a complete circle. That helps it spot stingrays on the sea floor. When a hammerhead spots a stingray, it uses its head to hold its prey down while it bites.

Basking shark

Basking Shark

This shark spends most of its time swimming on the surface of the water. It keeps its huge mouth open to suck up water and food. Then it filters out the water and eats the tiny **zooplankton** that remain. The basking shark is the second largest fish. They can grow up to 45 feet (14 meters) long and weigh up to five tons.

Wobbegong Shark

"Wobbegong" is an Australian **Aboriginal** word that means "shaggy." This shark gets its name from the long whiskers and flaps of skin on its face. Another name for this creature is the carpet shark, because it lies on the bottom of the ocean floor. They live in shallow water around the coast of Australia, Indonesia, and Japan.

Wobbegong shark

Mako Shark

Mako sharks live far out in the ocean. They are the fastest shark in the world. A shortfin mako swims faster than 31 miles (50 km) an hour. Their speed lets these sharks sneak up on their prey. Shortfin makos° can also jump 30 feet (9 meters) out of the water.

Mako shark

Thresher Shark

A thresher shark has an amazing tail. Its tail is almost as long as the shark's body. A thresher's tail helps it move quickly through the water. It also thrashes its tail around in a school of fish. This stuns its prey so the thresher can gobble them up.

Warning! Danger Ahead!

Sharks are amazing and important creatures. They keep the ocean healthy. They keep populations in balance by eating lots of fish and sea creatures. Most sharks never attack humans. They are not that scary.

However, some sharks do attack people. Usually sharks don't attack on purpose. The shark thinks a swimmer is a seal or another prey animal. It takes a bite, then realizes it made a mistake.

Now You Know!

Most shark attacks take place in the ocean. But in 1916, a shark swam up a creek in New Jersey and killed two people! Earlier, it had killed two swimmers on the ocean shore. The shark was later caught and killed in a nearby bay.

If you see shark warnings, stay out of the water!

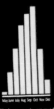

BE SHARK SMART
Great white sharks frequent these waters.

In emergencies
CALL 911

Peak Activity
Based on tagging data

May June July Aug Sep Oct Nov Dec

[Sharks may remain year-round]

Know your risk when entering the water.

Download the Sharktivity App to receive alerts and report sightings.
For more info and to view the latest research, visit: www.atlanticwhiteshark.org

NPS/Bill Fisher

Staying Safe From Sharks

It's important to be shark-safe if you are swimming in the ocean. Most sharks hunt at night, so it is safer to swim during the day. It's also safer to swim in a group and not by yourself.

Some beaches in Australia and South Africa put up nets to keep sharks from getting too close to shore. Lifeguards also watch out for sharks. Be sure to listen to guards and get out of the water if they say it's not safe.

Sharks in Trouble

Sharks are big and tough, but here's a scary fact. Sharks are in trouble! Fishing kills more than 100 million sharks each year. Some sharks are killed for their meat. Some are killed for sport. Other sharks die when they get caught in fishing nets.

Water pollution is also bad for sharks. Sharks will swallow almost anything. Some die after swallowing trash in the ocean. Pollution also damages the places where sharks live. Pollution kills their prey. Without a safe home and food to eat, sharks don't have a chance.

Now You Know!

Japan, Korea, Australia, New Zealand, India, and Iceland are just a few of the countries where the population regularly eats shark meat.

Millions of sharks die each year from getting tangled in fishing nets.

Learn more about sharks at an aquarium.

Helping Sharks

There are lots of ways to help sharks. Some governments ban shark fishing. You can do your part by keeping the ocean clean. Never leave trash on the beach or in the water. Learn all you can about sharks and the ocean. Tell people that sharks aren't scary. They are awesome!

FUN FACT: Some scientists tag sharks with special electronic IDs. They can track the shark and learn more about how it lives and where it goes.

Glossary

Aboriginal having to do with Australia's native people

cartilage flexible connecting tissue, unlike bone which is not flexible

filters removes things from water

gills organs on a fish's side through which it breathes

parasites creatures that get their food by living on or inside another animal or plant

predators animals that hunt other animals for food

prey animals that are hunted by other animals for food

species a group of living things of the same kind

zooplankton very tiny sea animals

Learn More in the Library

Claybourne, Anna. *Sharks: Predators of the Sea*. Firefly Books, 2016.

Jenkins, Steve. *The Shark Book*. Houghton Mifflin Harcourt, 2021.

Lowery, Mike. *Everything Awesome About Sharks and Other Underwater Creatures!* Orchard Books, 2020.

Pembroke, Ethan. *The Shark Encyclopedia for Kids*. Abdo Reference, 2021.

Index

About the Author

Joanne Mattern is the author of many books for children including the previous three sets of *Core Content: Earth's Amazing Animals Series.* She loves writing about sports, all kinds of animals, and interesting people. Mattern lives in New York State with her family.